ZAPiRO
Let the Sunshine In

Cartoons from *Daily Maverick and Sunday Times*

JACANA

Acknowledgements: Thanks to my editors at Daily Maverick *(Branko Brkic and Marianne Thamm) for brainstorm breakfasts and their key role in bringing down the Zupta cabal; thanks to my editors at the* Sunday Times *(Bongani Siqoko, S'Thembiso Msomi and many other astute editors I worked under for 20 years); thanks to all online and print production staff; thanks to Mike Wills for steering the way so soon after WTF; my trusty assistant Eleanora Bresler; Richard Hainebach for website management; Bridget Impey and all at Jacana; Claudine Willatt-Bate for layout; and as always, the home team − Nomalizo Ndlazi and my family, Karina, Tevya and Nina.*

10 Orange Street
Sunnyside
Auckland Park 2092
South Africa
(+27 11) 628 3200
www.jacana.co.za

in association with

P R O D U C T I O N S

ISBN 978-1-4314-2731-4

Cover design by Jonathan Shapiro
Page layout by Claudine Willatt-Bate
Job no. 003405

See a complete list of Jacana titles at www.jacana.co.za
See Zapiro's list and archive at www.zapiro.com

Printed by **novus print**, a Novus Holdings company

For error enders and course correctors

ZAPIRO annuals

The Madiba Years (1996)
The Hole Truth (1997)
End of Part One (1998)
Call Mr Delivery (1999)
The Devil Made Me Do It! (2000)
The ANC Went in 4x4 (2001)
Bushwhacked (2002)
Dr Do-Little and the African Potato (2003)
Long Walk to Free Time (2004)
Is There a Spin Doctor In the House? (2005)
Da Zuma Code (2006)
Take Two Veg and Call Me In the Morning (2007)
Pirates of Polokwane (2008)
Don't Mess With the President's Head (2009)
Do You Know Who I Am?! (2010)
The Last Sushi (2011)
But Will It Stand Up In Court? (2012)
My Big Fat Gupta Wedding (2013)
It's Code Red! (2014)
Rhodes Rage (2015)
Dead President Walking (2016)
Hasta la Gupta, baby! (2017)

Other books

The Mandela Files (2008)
VuvuzelaNation (2013)
DemoCrazy (2014)
WTF: capturing Zuma − a cartoonist's tale (2018)

Zuma acolyte and North West premier Supra Mahumapelo orders the erection
of a monument near Groot Marico where Zuma was arrested by apartheid police
in 1963. Without a hint of irony, the billboard reads 'Jacob Zuma Capture Site'.

6 October 2017

Tragic life of President Zuma's rape accuser is powerfully
told by author and popular talk show host Redi Tlhabi

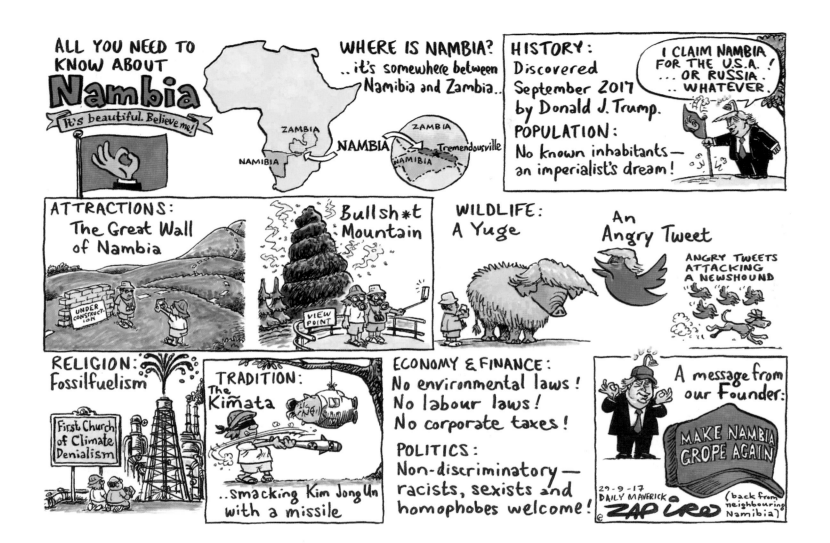

Speaking at the UN to African leaders, US President
Donald Trump twice refers to a country called Nambia

Yet another mass shooting in the US and the deadliest yet –
59 people attending a country music festival in Las Vegas are killed
by retiree Stephen Paddock who fired more than 1 000 rounds

4 October 2017

Rebel ANC MP lambastes the faction-driven party and leaves

8 October 2017

Posturing police minister's habitual bully-boy bluster on social media

He's so upset by my cartoon that he fills in the blank space with actions
he says he's taken – but won't explain an overseas trip reportedly
bankrolled by a sporting goods company when he was sports minister

10 October 2017

Now he boasts about being on the scene of a Western Cape 'midnight criminal space shake-up'.
Turns out the 'suspects' were taking a coffin back to the Eastern Cape for burial and were left
bound on the ground for hours waiting for Mbalula to show up ... and then they were all released.

17 October 2017

12 October 2017   Famous movie mogul faces a barrage of sexual assault and harassment allegations

SITTING PRESIDENT

15-10-17 SUN-TIMES

ZAPIRO

15 October 2017

Supreme Court confirms that the NPA's 2009 decision not to prosecute Zuma
was irrational and orders the prosecuting authority to reconsider the charges

18 October 2017

Zuma reshuffles his cabinet – this time without party approval. SACP boss Blade Nzimande is out and loyal allies David Mahlobo and Bongani Bongo get key positions.

Mahlobo is now at the energy ministry presumably to drive through the
monstrous nuclear deal with Russia which is expected to deliver kickbacks all round

24 October 2017

Mother city facing the mother of all water crises

22 October 2017

Still no legal action against Zuma, his family or the Guptas
but widespread probes are under way in the US and Britain

A dandy of note, Gupta-linked finance minister Malusi Gigaba
delivers the medium-term budget financial statement

25 October 2017

TRIPARTITE FRIGHT NIGHT

29 October 2017   Halloween is upon us as the alliance's internal strife heats up

2 November 2017

Soccer boss and former PE mayor Danny Jordaan stays silent
after singer and ex-ANC MP Jennifer Ferguson says he raped her

Parliament's Standing Committee on Public Accounts loses patience with
social development minister Bathabile Dlamini who's still distributing social grants via
CPS long after the ConCourt ruled the contract awarded to the company was irregular

3 November 2017

State Security Agency and SARS legally threaten author Jacques Pauw after his explosive book about Zuma and his crooked backers is published. It becomes an instant bestseller.

12 November 2017

15 November 2017

Carl Niehaus, who resigned as government spokesman in disgrace eight years ago,
surfaces alongside Nkosazana Dlamini-Zuma during her campaign for the party presidency
and achieves social media fame for some dodgy dance moves at a Jacob Zuma speech

7 November 2017

8 November 2017

The global hashtag for victims of sexual violence and harassment gets traction in SA.
Meanwhile the legal system takes strain from Zuma's constant challenges.

HEHER REPORT   HEH HEH REPORT

For months Zuma has sat on the findings of his own commission into student funding.
Now he arbitrarily announces free university education – on the advice of
an activist who was a campus spy and dated one of his daughters.

14 November 2017

ZIMBABWEAN GOTHIC

ZAPIRO
(after Grant Wood)
DAILY MAVERICK
10-11-17

Mnangagwa

PRESI-DENCY

10 November 2017

93-year-old Robert Mugabe axes his vice-president, Emmerson Mnangagwa.
The ZANU-PF Youth Wing calls for Mugabe's wife Grace to take the position.

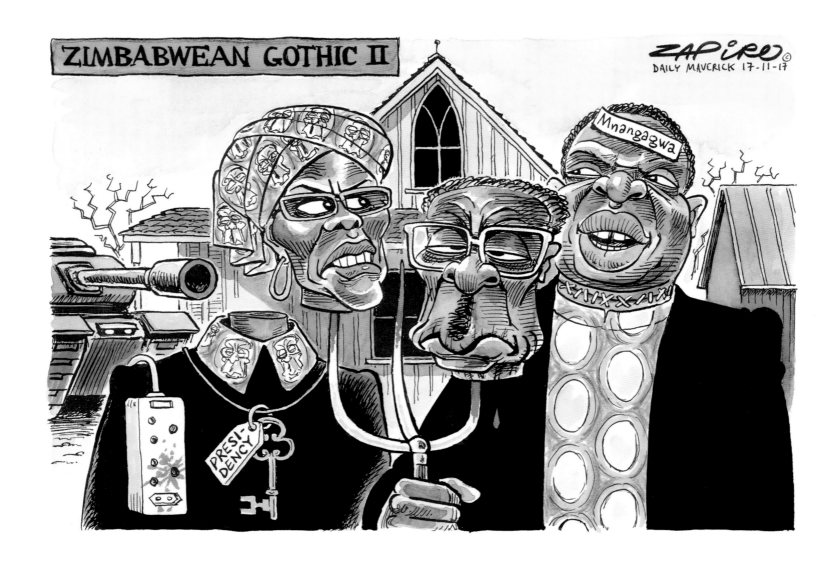

ZIMBABWEAN GOTHIC II

ZAPiRO
DAILY MAVERICK 17-11-17

Mnangagwa, known as the Crocodile, fights back –
he places Mugabe and his wife under house arrest but says it isn't a coup

17 November 2017

21 November 2017   Mugabe continues to ignore deadlines for his 'voluntary' departure

22 November 2017

He resigns after 37 years in power as the Zim
parliament begins impeachment proceedings against him

26 November 2017   New strongman sworn in

Guptas' favourite CEO Brian Molefe is grilled in parliament about
his R30m Eskom payout while the SA National Defence Union cries
foul about the army giving him a paid job as an unqualified officer

23 November 2017

34

Two Cabinet ministers duck grilling in parliament because they're sick. The Life Esidimeni inquiry into the deaths of 143 mentally ill patients is also experiencing medical no-shows.

3 December 2017

5 December 2017

ANC leadership battle goes down to the wire. With 11 days to go,
Cyril Ramaphosa seems to have a slight edge over Nkosazana Dlamini-Zuma.

Billionaire Naspers boss denies that millions paid to the SABC and the Guptas' ANN7 channel were part of a plan to gain influence over government broadcasting policies

6 December 2017

37

8 December 2017

Trump goes through with his campaign promise to recognise
Jerusalem as Israel's capital and to move the US embassy to the city

Pretoria High Court rules that Zuma's appointment of Shaun 'The Sheep' Abrahams as NPA head was invalid because his dismissal of Abrahams's predecessor, Mxolisi Nxasana, was unlawful. The court orders deputy president Ramaphosa to decide on a new prosecution head as Zuma is conflicted.

10 December 2017

© ZAPIRO DAILY MAVERICK 13-12-17

Steinhoff CEO and prominent racehorse owner Markus Jooste
is the man behind SA's biggest-ever corporate scandal

13 December 2017

40

Rejecting Zuma's appeal against Thuli Madonsela's State Capture report
as ill-advised and reckless, the North Gauteng High Court slaps him with
personal cost orders and prescribes the urgent appointment of a judicial inquiry

14 December 2017

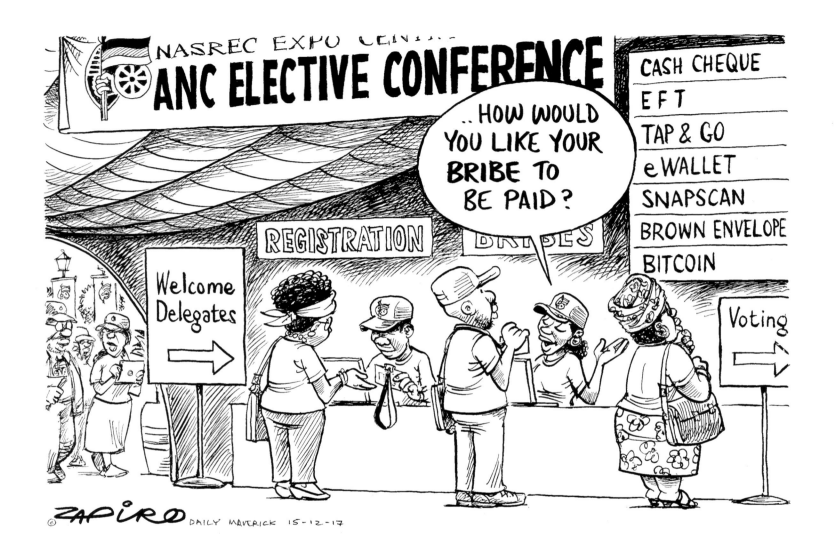

15 December 2017

The ANC conference at NASREC in Soweto, which will elect a new party leader, is beset by rumours of delegates, and even entire delegations, being bought off

19 December 2017   Cyril Ramaphosa defeats Nkosazana Dlamini-Zuma by a mere 179 votes

ANOTHER ANC
TOXSIX MIX

DAILY MAVERICK 20·12·17 ZAPIRO

TOXSIX ASSETS

TOXSIX WASTE

Ramaphosa's victory is tarnished by the election of tainted rivals David Mabuza,
Ace Magashule and Jessie Duarte into the party's top six leadership group

20 December 2017

21 December 2017   Reports of missing and wrongly disqualified votes which could have changed conference outcomes

2017 ABC

ZAPIRO
SUN. TIMES 24-12-17

A's for Accounting (not covered in glory)

B is Bell Pottinger's similar story

C is how Cyril sort of won the great race

D — Dlamini-Zuma disappeared without trace

E is for Eskom, their noses keep growing

F — Finance ministers coming and going

G is for Guptas, the empire's leaking

H is for Hashtag, survivors are speaking

I's Impeachment avoidance, he's tried every trick

J is for Judges — make those charges stick!

K's Khwezi's story in case you forgot it

L is for Literacy — Grade 4s aint got it

M is Mugabe, finally booted

N's NPA — Shaun the Sheep has been neutered

O — Oscar's jailed longer despite all his pleading

P — Jacques Pauw's book has got us all reading

Q's Question time circus, EFF versus Speaker

R — SA Rugby got stronger and weaker

S — Saxonwold's State Capture Shebeen

T is for Trump — worst Prez ever seen

U — Universities, protests on campus

V — 68 Votes gone missing caused ANC rumpus

W — Water crisis, the Cape's current plight

X — Xenophobia, a nationwide blight

Y no Hawks arrests? Crooks just dived and ducked

Z is still Zuma — till he's gone we're still f*#@#&!!

24 December 2017

Zuma and his cabal in the NEC dig in and frustrate
Ramaphosa's attempts to remove him from office

12 January 2018

SHITHOLE UTTERANCE

14 January 2018

Questioning immigration from Africa, Trump asks why more people 'from shithole countries' should be allowed into the USA

Global clothing chain's advert tagging a black child 'clever monkey'
sparks outrage and the Malema-fuelled trashing of several stores

17 January 2018

Stalling his now-inevitable departure, he's making demands about cabinet posts for his allies
and asking for a long delay to introduce Ramaphosa to his 'friends' in the BRICS countries

ANOTHER FROZEN GUPTA ASSET

thanks Errol C.
SUN.TIMES 21-1-18

ZAPIRO

21 January 2018   The Asset Forfeiture Unit freezes the assets of 14 people and entities linked to Gupta deals

Blame-shifting officials at former deputy chief justice Dikgang Moseneke's inquiry
into the fatal transfers of Gauteng mental health patients from the Life Esidimeni facility

23 January 2018

18 January 2018

A leaked internal report on Cape Town mayor Patricia de Lille's administration is now a party headache for leader Mmusi Maimane

24 January 2018

Still not president, Ramaphosa heads for the World Economic Forum in Switzerland

28 January 2018

Ahead of Judge Zondo's State Capture inquiry, the Hawks execute search and seizure operations linking mining minister Mosebenzi Zwane and Free State premier Ace Magashule to a scheme by the Guptas and Duduzane Zuma that milked millions out of a dairy farm project

President Trump's One Year in Office

Africa
Muslims
Gays
Immigrants
Media
Women
World Peace
Mexico
Climate
Health Care
Palestine
Gun Control
Europe

ANUS HORRIBILIS

30-1-18 DAILY MAVERICK
thanks Helen W.

30 January 2018

Magashule calls Zuma a 'wonderful president' and Duarte says he'll serve his full term

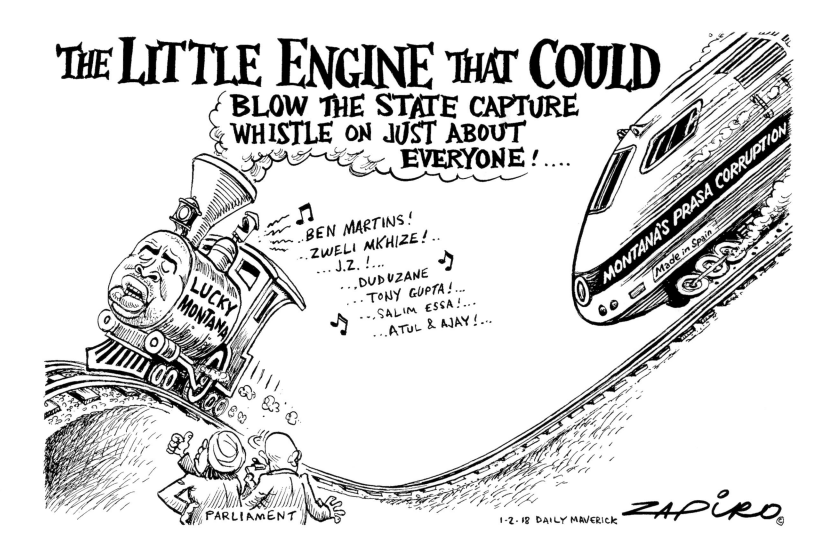

While former Passenger Rail Agency CEO Lucky Montana explosively names names during the parliamentary Eskom inquiry, his own actions in Spanish train purchases are being seriously questioned

1 February 2018

4 February 2018   Springbok rugby coach Allister Coetzee axed after a drawn-out process

6 February 2018   Still he clings on, adamant that he will deliver the State of the Nation address in a week's time

7 February 2018

DAY ZERO

Cape Town is counting down to the day the city runs out of water

11 February 2018   Unprecedented postponement of SONA while the ANC wrestles with Zuma's exit

FREEDOM CELEBRATION

13 February 2018

Speaking at Cape Town's City Hall, where he famously stood
alongside Madiba in 1990, Cyril launches the icon's centenary year

14 February 2018

The end of an error

15 February 2018   The party recalls Zuma and he finally accepts his fate in a rambling, self-pitying late-night speech

18 February 2018

Cyril is sworn in and delivers an upbeat SONA vowing to tackle
corruption and launching his Thuma Mina ('send me') campaign

Mayor De Lille is another who's been clinging to office and
now her party blames her for mismanaging Cape Town's water woes

Malusi Gigaba delivers the budget but is widely rumoured
to be facing the axe along with many compromised ministers

23 February 2018

25 February 2018

The court ordered him out of the NPA but Abrahams has appealed and now he says he is applying his mind to the decision to prosecute Zuma or not

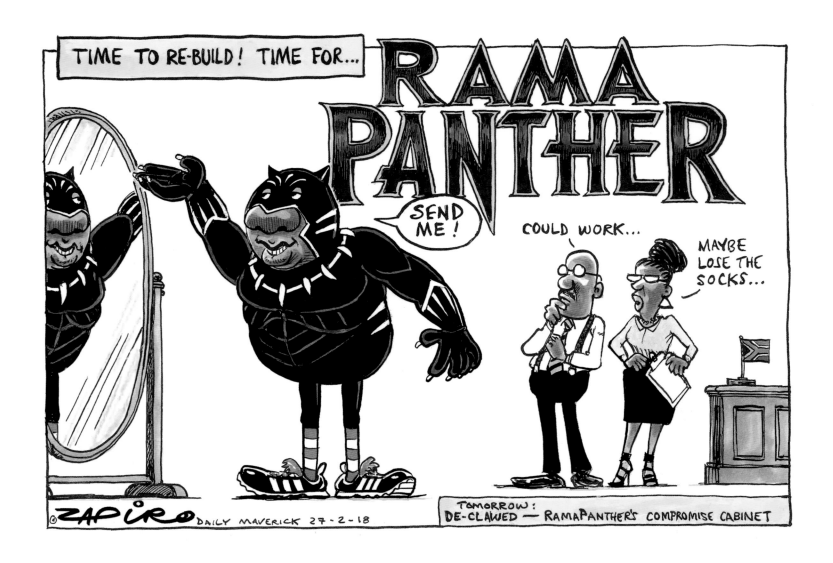

27 February 2018   *Black Panther* is the movie sensation of the year

Cyril announces his cabinet, firing some tainted figures but retaining others
like Gigaba (shifted back to home affairs) and Bathabile Dlamini who
famously defended Zuma by claiming everyone had their little secrets to hide

28 February 2018

73

Land grab

Without Zuma to shout about, Malema's been making land his main talking point.
So the ruling party makes an abrupt policy shift in parliament.

2 March 2018

SAXONWOLD SHEBEEN'S Academy of State Capture Arts & Sciences presents

THE LAST ZUPTA AWARDS

BEST ACTOR:
Brian Molefe
Runners-up:
Anoj Singh, Ace Magashule

BEST ACTRESS:
Lynne Brown
for 'I knew nothing!'

BEST PERFORMANCE IN A SUPPORTING ROLE (shared):
KPMG, McKinsey, SAP, Bank of Baroda, Jimmy Manyi, Jesse Duarte, Moegsien Williams, Andile Mngxitama

BEST SCRIPT:
Bell Pottinger for
'White Monopoly Capital'

BEST EDITING:
The (new) Public Protector's various Zuptafied reports

BEST SONG:
Nazeem Howa for
'7000 will be jobless' Blues

BEST PROSTHETICS:
Minister Zwane's
ever-growing nose

BEST COMEDY PERFORMANCE:
ANN7
and Shaun the Sheep

BEST NON-PERFORMANCE:
Tom Moyane
for SARS

BEST FOREIGN FEATURE: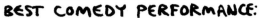
The Guptas for
'Bought a country, what a bargain!'

BEST DIRECTING:
The Guptas for
'**We** pick J.Z.'s Cabinet'

BEST SPECIAL EFFECTS:
Duduzane Zuma for
disappearing act ('Time to say Dubai')

BEST STUNT:
Atul Gupta drops in
at SA's Dubai embassy

BEST SHORT ANIMATION:
Malusi GiGupta in
'I'm no Zupta!'

BEST PICTURE:
J.Z. behind bars
(forthcoming attraction)

Sun.Times 4-3-18

ZAPIRO

3 March 2018

Remember me? I'm Sam-I-am!
I made him eat green eggs and ham
unaware that Tiger Brands'
testing process was a sham!
New labelling (this is not hysteria):
'PROCESSED MEAT — CONTAINS LISTERIA'

homage to Dr Seuss   DAILY MAVERICK 7-3-18   ZAPIRO

7 March 2018   Health Department links deadly listeria outbreak to meat products made by Tiger Brands

8 March 2018

More ministers and officials duck accountability at hearings on State Capture

14 March 2018   The normally cocky Gigaba cuts a hapless figure at the inquiry

13 March 2018   The official opposition sends out an alarmist text about expropriation without compensation

STEPHEN HAWKING
1942 – 2018

cosmologist, communicator,
barrier breaker

15 March 2018

18 March 2018

Missing in action for years, prosecutions boss Abrahams says Zuma will stand trial for
16 charges involving 783 incidents of racketeering, money laundering, corruption and fraud

APARTHEID HOME AFFAIRS MINISTERS

1920s - '30s

D.F. MALAN

1970s

CONNIE MULDER

1980s

STOFFEL BOTHA

2018

Australia's PETER DUTTON

FAST-TRACK VISAS FOR WHITE S.A. FARMERS

20 March 2018

Aussie cabinet minister says persecuted white South African farmers
deserve special attention and 'need help from a civilized country like ours'

21 March 2018   The president suspends SARS boss Tom Moyane when he refuses to step down

EFF deputy president Floyd Shivambu grabs News24 photographer
by the throat, demands he delete pictures and tries to break his camera

23 March 2018

Disgraced Steinhoff boss refuses to appear before parliamentary committees.
The Gupta brothers, former SAA chair Dudu Myeni and Duduzane Zuma
are threatened with summonses if they don't turn up at hearings

28 March 2018

4 April 2018

Winnie Madikizela-Mandela dies leaving a complex and contested legacy

ACE-COME-LATELY

11 April 2018

At memorial service for Winnie, ANC stalwart Trevor Manuel lashes Ace Magashule and says funds meant to convert her Brandfort house into a museum have been diverted elsewhere

5 April 2018

10 April 2018

Claiming he's been persecuted and betrayed, Zuma
threatens to spill the beans on those besmirching his name

Media mogul tries, and fails, to list his hopelessly overblown media company despite the best efforts of his Independent Newspapers praise-singers

12 April 2018

18 April 2018

The State Security Agency director general was a key intelligence operative for Zuma. Ramaphosa abruptly moves him to the prisons department.

19 April 2018

Two judges – Nkola Motata and John Hlophe –
have pulled every trick to avoid facing up to long-standing charges

20 April 2018   Disastrous provincial premier won't resign, nor will the president fire him

Kaizer Chiefs fans react violently to Nedbank Cup loss in Durban,
beating up a security guard on the pitch and causing millions of rands damage

25 April 2018   Court rejects claim for damages sought by the family of a five-year-old boy who drowned in faeces

26 April 2018

Zwelinzima Vavi's new SA Federation of Trade Unions
launches its first national protests over the minimum wage

Global athletics body appears to target Olympic gold medallist Caster Semenya
through new rules for athletes with 'difference of sexual development'
only applicable in 400m, 800m and 1500m races

1 May 2018

Unfazed after losing a motion of no confidence, she insists
on 'due process' and demands an open disciplinary hearing

8 May 2018 · *Avengers: Infinity War* is the latest super-hero movie

Supra-factionalistic-egocentric-and-verbocious

Jesus-complex premier Gupta-linked and quite atrocious

Said he'd quit but backtracked with a faction-fuelled psychosis

Supra-testing ruling party's top-down power sclerosis!

N.E.C.

HANDS OFF SUPRA!

North West Prov

RamaPoppins!

DAILY MAVERICK
11·5·18
ZAPIRO

11 May 2018

Pretoria places North West Province under administration. Embattled premier
Supra Mahumapelo resigns, then withdraws his resignation and vows to fight on.

More than 50 Palestinian protesters die as the US embassy
is controversially relocated to Jerusalem – a moment hailed by
prime minister Benjamin Netanyahu as a 'glorious day for Israel'

16 May 2018

SuperSport analyst and former Springbok Ashwin Willemse dramatically
walks out on a live broadcast saying he 'will not be patronised' by colleagues
Nick Mallett and Naas Botha 'who played their rugby during the apartheid era'

22 May 2018

"...the essence of the absence of presence"
—SUPRA MAHUMAPELO

ZAPIRO
DAILY MAVERICK
24-5-18

PREMIER-SHIP

ANC PROVINCIAL CHAIRMANSHIP

N.W. PROVINCE

24 May 2018

He makes an inscrutable statement and resigns as premier
but retains the provincial party leadership

30 May 2018

Widely-reported rape allegations against Danny Jordaan haven't prevented
his resounding re-election as South African Football Association head

Court cites lack of evidence and orders immediate return
of R250m of assets frozen in the Estina dairy farm case

31 May 2018

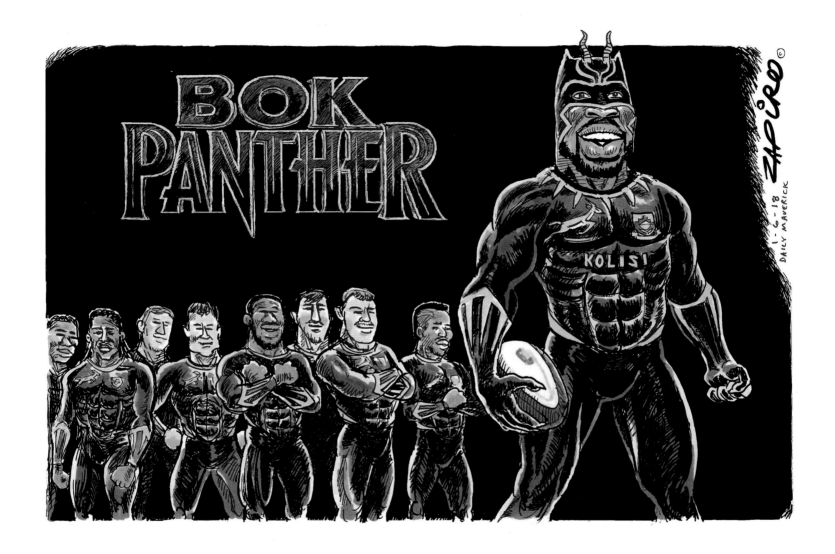

1 June 2018

Siya Kolisi becomes national rugby team's first-ever black captain

The DA has suspended her membership and given her mayoral duties
to Ian Neilson but Patricia defiantly heads to the courts

5 June 2018

At every turn Zuma and his supporters resist the new leadership.
He's even rumoured to be starting his own party.

6 June 2018

RENAMING QUESTIONNAIRE

I think Cape Town International Airport should be called:

- ☐ Nelson Mandela International
- ☐ Ahmed Kathrada International
- ☐ Sara Baartman International
- ☐ Krotoa International
- ☐ Robert Sobukwe International
- * ☐ Joe Masepus International

* RECEIVING RUSH OF LOCAL SUPPORT

DAILY MAVERICK 7·6-18 ZAPIRO ©
apology and thanks to the wit who posted Joe M. on social media

Kallie Kriel says not enough people were killed under apartheid for it to be called a crime against humanity. Floyd Shivambu is blatantly stirring anti-Indian sentiment. The SA Sevens team take the world title and the Springboks get a thrilling win over England on the same weekend.

12 June 2018

13 June 2018   Kim Jong-un and Trump meet in Singapore

Pubic Protector Busisiwe Mkhwebane delivers yet another fatally flawed report
— this time on Western Cape premier Helen Zille's tweets

15 June 2018

20 June 2018

BLUSTER'S LAST STAND

4 July 2018

Tom Moyane makes the false claim that two different inquiries digging
into his tainted tenure as head of SARS represent unfair double jeopardy

Bewildering party appointments

Traditional leaders coining it and resisting rural land tenure rights are 'village tinpot dictators',
says the ANC's Kgalema Motlanthe. Zulu King Goodwill Zwelithini, backed by
IFP leader Mangosuthu Buthelezi, vows to fight any interference.

6 July 2018

With the Guptas safely in Dubai following serial inaction on State Capture, the NPA celebrates charging Zuma's son Duduzane — more than two years after the evidence was first made public — over his involvement in the Guptas' attempt to bribe former deputy finance minister Mcebisi Jonas

10 July 2018

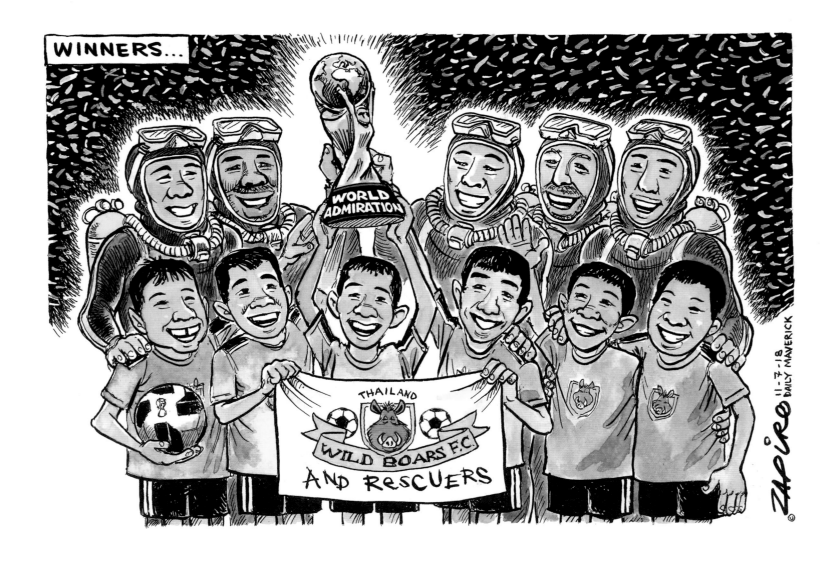

Astonishing rescue of Thai youth soccer team from flooded caves
gets massive global attention even during FIFA World Cup

17 July 2018

Fielding many players of multi-cultural origin, France beat
plucky underdogs Croatia 4–2 to lift the biggest trophy in sport

DAILY MAVERICK 12-7-18
thanks Qaanitah H. & Mike W. ZAPIRO ©

12 July 2018   Zuma ditches his long-standing legal advisor and finds a new one

In his lecture to mark the centenary of Nelson Mandela's birth,
Barack Obama calls on the world to resist the politics of fear and resentment

18 July 2018

MORAL COMPASS

MORAL WINDVANE

Centenary special: Half-learnt lessons from Madiba

Mahlangu was accountable for 144 deaths in the Life Esidimeni scandal.
Hlongwa was implicated in a massive corruption probe.
Both get elected onto the party's provincial exco.

25 July 2018

30 July 2018

Zimbabwe goes to the polls

Aggressive new kid on the political block turns five

2 August 2018

The economy's ailing — not helped by Ramaphosa's sudden late-night
announcement on land policy — so there's yet another half-baked revival plan

7 August 2018

Patricia and Mmusi reach a secretly negotiated agreement — he drops
the disciplinary proceedings against her and she'll resign in three months' time

Convicted of assaulting women at nightclubs and also facing charges of physically abusing a domestic worker, former deputy minister Mduduzi Manana remains an ANC MP and is advertised as a panellist at a fundraiser for women who are victims of violence

8 August 2018

The *New York Times* details new deputy president David Mabuza's rise
to power through years of corruption and inflating party membership lists
while presiding over a murderous political climate in Mpumalanga

10 August 2018

ConCourt confirms that Zuma's axing of NPA boss Mxolisi Nxasana
was unlawful and that Shaun Abrahams's subsequent appointment
was invalid. The president is given 90 days to find a replacement.

14 August 2018

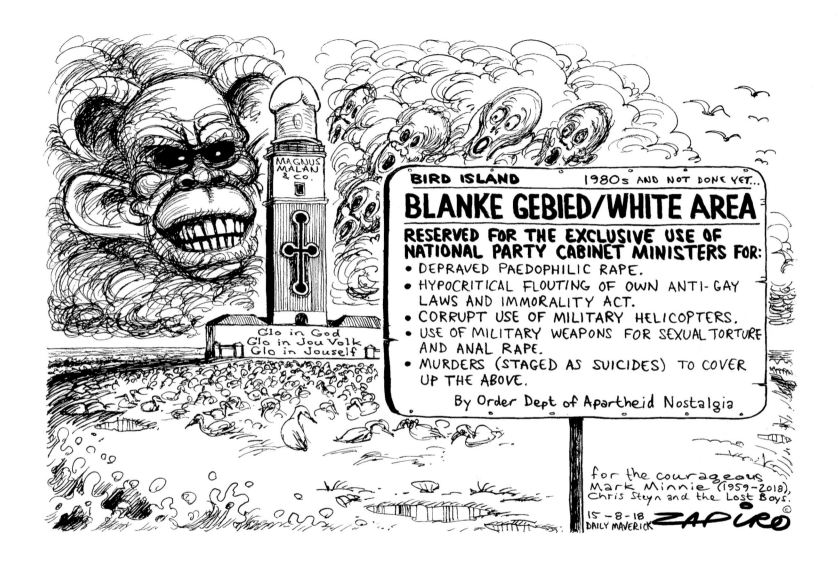

The cartoon text reads:

BIRD ISLAND — 1980s AND NOT DONE YET...

BLANKE GEBIED/WHITE AREA

RESERVED FOR THE EXCLUSIVE USE OF NATIONAL PARTY CABINET MINISTERS FOR:

- DEPRAVED PAEDOPHILIC RAPE.
- HYPOCRITICAL FLOUTING OF OWN ANTI-GAY LAWS AND IMMORALITY ACT.
- CORRUPT USE OF MILITARY HELICOPTERS.
- USE OF MILITARY WEAPONS FOR SEXUAL TORTURE AND ANAL RAPE.
- MURDERS (STAGED AS SUICIDES) TO COVER UP THE ABOVE.

By Order Dept of Apartheid Nostalgia

MAGNUS MALAN & CO.

Glo in God
Glo in Jou Volk
Glo in Jouself

for the courageous Mark Minnie (1959-2018), Chris Steyn and the Lost Boys.
15-8-18 DAILY MAVERICK ZAPIRO

15 August 2018

Mark Minnie, former PE cop and co-author of a devastating book about appalling behaviour by Nat cabinet ministers, is found dead from apparent suicide … but many are suspicious

Aretha Franklin − Queen of Soul, civil rights champion
and friend of Martin Luther King − passes away

17 August 2018

Deputy Chief Justice Raymond Zondo gets his long-awaited
commission under way with grumbles that government agencies
are not co-operating and lawyers are constantly delaying

21 August 2018

23 August 2018

Responding to an alarmist Fox News report, the US president tweets
inaccurately and simplistically about SA land seizures and farm killings

24 August 2018

Double standards? The EFF has slammed State Capture yet party chair Dali Mpofu
attacks Pravin Gordhan and aggressively defends Tom Moyane at the inquiry
into the disastrous decline of SARS under Moyane's watch.

28 August 2018

100 years after the sinking of the troopship *Mendi,* with the loss
of more than 600 mostly black SA troops, British Prime Minister
Theresa May brings a gift to Pretoria during her state visit

29 August 2018

5 September 2018   Finance minister tries to calm the nation after grim data

7 September 2018

The Guptas are prepared to give evidence to the Zondo Commission – and want to cross-examine witnesses – but only via video from their Middle East bolt-hole

Sunday Times reveals a clandestine Durban meeting between
Zuma and his allies Dudu Myeni, Ace Magashule, Supra Mahumapelo,
ANC Youth League's Thanduxolo Sabelo and the Women's League's Meokgo Matuba

11 September 2018

13 September 2018

After initial denials by ANC spokespeople, Magashule owns up to
the Zuma meeting first reported by Qaanitah Hunter in the *Sunday Times*

The president addresses the 13th national congress
of the shrinking and increasingly off-the-pace union federation

18 September 2018

19 September 2018

ConCourt upholds Western Cape High Court decision
that the personal use of cannabis is not a criminal offence

BAD COP, JUST-AS-BAD COP

At the Zondo Commission, major banks confirm they were not only bullied by captured minister Mosebenzi Zwane but also pressured by ANC worthies like Gwede Mantashe to do business with the Guptas

21 September 2018

25 September 2018   Just as the president talks up the details of his recovery plan …

The minister now downgraded back to Home Affairs is forced to fix his own mess – absurd child
visa restrictions ruining tourism. He stubbornly won't scrap them completely and explodes
on Twitter over reports that his own messy family life triggered the rules in the first place.

28 September 2018

UNVEILING...

NELSON MANDELA

UNITED NATION

GUTERRES

JACOB ZUMA

ZAPIRO thanks Mike W.
DAILY MAVERICK 27-9-18

27 September 2018   The world cements Madiba's stature, Cyril doing the honours